MATRICULATION

BORROWING
WHILE **BLACK**

DR. TISA SILVER CANADY

ISBN: 978-1-7343339-5-4

PACKAGE YOUR GENIUS
BOOKS

SHERRILYN LAVERNE SMITH SILVER
B.S. Accounting
Virginia State University
Class of 1969
Hometown: Ruther Glen, VA

"I received a scholarship from VSU of $200 per year for being ranked #4 in my high school class. College cost about $800 per year. One year, I missed a financial aid deadline for paperwork and had to ask my dad to give me $900. He did. I graduated with $2,400 in student loans and I think the interest rates were around 2 or 3 percent. Textbooks may have cost $5."

dedication

TO MOM AND DAD:
I REMAIN IN AWE OF YOUR MANY SUCCESSES
AND IN GRATITUDE FOR THE BENEFITS I ENJOY BECAUSE OF THEM.

There was a country girl whose brains matched her beauty. She grew up in the segregated South with her elementary education completed in a one-room schoolhouse. She excelled in school and went to Virginia State University as a first-generation college student studying accounting. She graduated, began working in the federal government, transitioned to higher education, and rose to the rank of interim chief financial officer. She is the ultimate college success story. She never forgot her roots and led the initiative to have that small schoolhouse designated as a historic site in the Commonwealth of Virginia.

It pains me to speak of you in the past tense, my dear. Your legacy influences my path daily. Grace, faith, strength, integrity, self-advocacy...you were and always will be cherished, loved, and admired.

EZEL SILVER, JR.
B.S. Engineering
Howard University
Class of 1970
Hometown: Newark, NJ

"I received scholarships from Lockheed (before it became Lockheed Martin) and the Newark Evening News for delivering newspapers. My mother paid cash (much from her earnings as a part-time Avon saleswoman) and I worked summer jobs. I graduated without borrowing any student loans."

dedication

This young man's story began in a single-parent home in the projects of Newark, NJ. He ran a paper route during the day and was once robbed on that route, at knifepoint. By night, he returned to a one-bedroom apartment where he slept in the living room on a convertible bed. Yet still, he excelled in the classroom so much so that he graduated high school at the age of 16. His sights were set on a big out-of-state school not too far from home, but the color of his skin likely precluded that vision from taking shape. It was off to "The Mecca" instead where he became an electrical engineer. He returned to his alma mater to help build the student center and traveled the world as a diplomat practicing his craft.

In the world of girl dads, you reign supreme. Your generosity, humility, and consideration for others is an example I aspire to. I cannot thank you enough.

table of contents

introduction

In September 2019, I was active on Twitter chatting during the debut of the BET special "Young, Gifted and Broke." Soon after, a student from Howard University reached out to me via Twitter about contributing to an article on student loans and Black borrowers. I was happy to help! After jotting down my initial thoughts and opinions I searched for statistics to confirm or deny those opinions. I noticed a plethora of evidence pointing to disparities between Black and non-Black borrowers. The other thing I noticed was a paucity of tools. Don't get me wrong—there is plenty of great work taking place in the realm of research; however, I could not find a resource geared toward Black college students that laid out the facts and provided actions to help borrowers achieve more favorable outcomes. Perhaps greater awareness will spark greater action.

WHAT THIS BOOK IS NOT:

A solution for fixing the system that perpetuates the racial wealth gap. There are plenty of researchers working in this space (a short list is included at the end of this book). You will not see my name among them! I am a personal finance expert but I am new to this space. My contribution is not to the body of literature but to helping borrowers do what they can to avoid the outcomes I am about to share. There is a system in place—that did not begin with student loans—which has kept Black wealth lagging behind. The system needs fixing but individuals cannot wait on the system. You must do something.

WHAT THIS BOOK IS:

A concise compilation of five facts that capture outcomes associated with borrowing student loans while Black. Each fact is accompanied by an explanation in layman's terms and the long-term significance of the fact. After a summary, I provide recommendations to help students—current and future—achieve a better student loan outcome.

Finally, the recommendations at the end of this book are not just for Black borrowers; any borrower can benefit from them. Given the differences in outcomes for Black versus non-Black borrowers, I believe Black borrowers stand to gain the most from putting them into practice. My desire is for Black borrowers to adopt these recommendations en masse because a change in collective behavior will lead to a change in collective outcomes.

terms

ACCRUE

The process of interest being charged on the principal balance of a loan. Interest can accrue at different intervals depending on the terms of each loan. Some loans allow for interest to accrue once per year, whereas others may allow it to accrue as often as once per day.

FINANCING

Source(s) of funding used to pay for something. The term "financing" usually refers to borrowing a loan but sometimes it is used to include a mix of funding sources such as personal savings, gift money, and loans.

INTEREST

The price you pay, as a percentage on each dollar, for borrowing money. Think of simple interest as cents on the dollar. For instance, a 5% interest rate on a $100 loan means you would repay five cents on each dollar (.05 x $100) = $5 of interest.

MATRICULATE

To enroll as a student, usually in a college.

PRINCIPAL

Typically, the original amount of a loan. However, with certain types of loans —including student loans— unpaid interest can become principal. Once this happens, interest will start to grow on the new, higher principal.

Once you **MATRICULATE**, you will receive a bill from your school.
How will you pay? = **FINANCING**

"GIFT AID"
You do not have
to repay.

LOANS
How much will you
repay?

PRINCIPAL + **INTEREST**

Original amount
borrowed

The "price"
to borrow

HOW MUCH?
A percentage on
every dollar of
principal. Stated as
an annual rate, but
interest **ACCRUES**
every day.

THE OTHER "PRICE" TO BORROW

Student loans have another cost:
the origination fee. The fee is a
percentage of the principal
borrowed and is deducted before
the borrowed funds are posted to
your student account.
*Example: You borrowed $1,000.
Your student account shows a
disbursement of $980. The $20
difference represents a 2%
origination fee.*

How much interest accrues daily?

It depends on the amount of principal and the interest rate. A loan with a
6% interest rate will accrue 1.64 cents per $100 of principal per day.

PRINCIPAL BORROWED	DAILY INTEREST ACCRUED
$1,000	$0.16
$5,000	$0.82
$10,000	$1.64

fact:

BLACK STUDENTS BORROW MORE

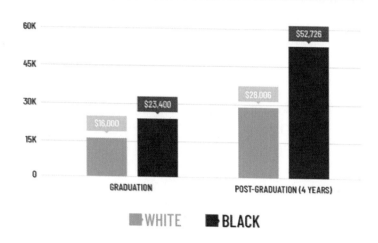

STUDENT LOAN DEBT
graduation vs. post-graduation (4 years)

	GRADUATION	POST-GRADUATION (4 YEARS)
WHITE	$16,000	$28,006
BLACK	$23,400	$52,726

Black graduates with bachelor's degrees owe $7,400 more student debt on average upon graduation than White graduates.[1]

WHY DOES IT MATTER?

Borrowing more makes you responsible for repaying more. Using the Standard Repayment Plan (which requires a fixed monthly payment for 120 months), the Black graduate would be responsible to pay $77 more per month ($243 versus $166). This equates to $924 extra per year or $9,240 over the course of repayment. This extra amount assumes that all payments are made on time, in full, and without any breaks in repayment. The longer you take to repay, the larger the gap will become, and making late payments or missing payments will cause the gap to swell even more.

Four years after graduation, the overall student loan debt balance had risen for both Black and White graduates. However, the gap between the groups had widened to roughly $24,000. The debt of Black graduates was 125 percent higher than the original balance, compared to a 75 percent increase for White graduates. Now you can see that the $7,400 gap was just the beginning.

WHAT COULD YOU DO WITH AN EXTRA $7,400?

Buy a used car. Boost your savings. Put a down payment on your first house. In early 2020, you could purchase 20 or so shares of stock in Apple. Or you could pay down your student loan debt. Extra funds that must be paid toward student loans may prevent you from saving, spending, and/or investing. The bottom line is that having a higher level of debt can rob you of these opportunities and limits your choices; having less debt expands your choices.

If you are looking to purchase your first car or home, lenders will examine all of your debt, including student loans, to determine how much car or home they believe you can afford. If you need to borrow for an auto or home loan, then having more debt equates to having fewer options. As for saving and investing, having more debt means missing opportunities to build wealth.

fact:

BLACK STUDENTS BORROW MORE OFTEN

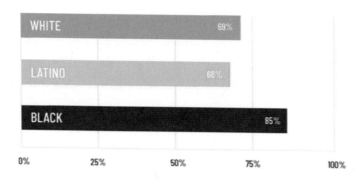

PERCENTAGE OF STUDENTS WHO BORROW
by race

WHITE	69%
LATINO	66%
BLACK	85%

0%   25%   50%   75%   100%

Eighty-five percent (85%) of Black bachelor's degree recipients borrowed student loans versus 69 percent of White students and 66 percent of Hispanic/Latino students.[2]

WHY DOES IT MATTER?

Black students generally come from households with lower wealth. They exhibit a greater level of financial need when applying for financial aid. During the 2019-2020 academic year, the maximum value of the Pell Grant (a need-based source of federal financial aid which does not have to be repaid) covered less than one-third of the average college expenses for attending a public, four-year university.[3] Student loans are therefore being used to cover the gaps. Higher rates of borrowing among students who come from households with lower income and wealth means that after college these students and their families will have an additional barrier to increasing wealth: student loan debt. In other words, Black households will continue to lag behind others in the accumulation of wealth.

WEALTH BY RACE

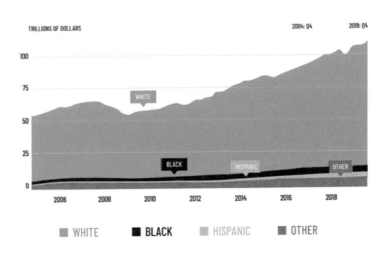

Source: Survey of Consumer Finances and Financial Accounts of the United States

"There's no financial literacy class that you can take to prepare for the fact that as a Black college graduate, no matter where you go — be it Ivy League, be it HBCU, be it PWI, be it private — you're more than likely to make less money in many cases than White college graduates."

– MICHAEL ARCENEAUX
  AUTHOR, *I DON'T WANT TO DIE POOR*

fact:

BLACK STUDENTS GRADUATE LESS OFTEN

SIX-YEAR COLLEGE COMPLETION RATES

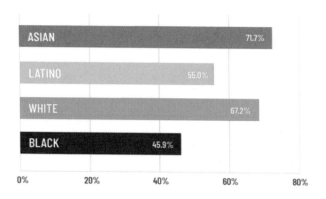

ASIAN	71.7%
LATINO	55.0%
WHITE	67.2%
BLACK	45.9%

Among students who started in four-year public institutions, Black students had the lowest six-year completion rate (45.9 percent). The completion rate of Hispanic students is 55 percent. Completion rates for White and Asian students are 67.2 percent and 71.7 percent, respectively.[4]

WHY DOES IT MATTER?

People who graduate from college typically earn more money throughout their lifetime than people who do not. Some researchers have estimated that earning a college degree boosts average lifetime earnings by $1 million.[5] The higher earnings potential comes with many costs (tuition and fees, room and board, etc.) and Black students tend to rely more heavily on student loans to cover those costs.

Student loans must be repaid regardless of whether you graduate, and leaving college without a degree means you must repay the loans without earning the higher income that comes along with earning a degree. All else held equal, having higher debt means less money available for saving or investing—again, limited choices. Finally, if you had little to no wealth going into college and left college without graduating, then you are likely to have even less wealth after college due to the new debt that you must repay.

"Black students
tend to come from
lower socioeconomic
backgrounds, have families
with little or no college
experience, and graduate
from underperforming
high schools that didn't
prepare them well for
higher education."

– CHRONICLE OF HIGHER EDUCATION
Sarah Brown, 02.14.2019

fact:

BLACK STUDENTS ARE MORE LIKELY TO EARN LESS

Today, young Black college graduates face a 16.8 percent pay penalty relative to their White counterparts.[6] The wage penalty is often larger for Black women.

WHY DOES IT MATTER?

The penalty at the start of your career often stays with you as you advance to higher paying positions. Employers typically ask job applicants to provide their salary history. Let's suppose you are applying for a new job and your most recent salary was $50,000. The employer may not share that the salary range for the new job is $65,000 to $75,000. Even though the upper limit is $75,000, they will probably offer you a salary on the lower end because of your existing salary. If they discriminate based on race and/or gender (yes, this still happens), then the offer may be reduced further. Your loss represents their savings. A career spent working at a discount can greatly limit your wealth-building potential over time.

Lower income likely means less money available to put toward buying assets (items of value) that may grow in value (appreciate) over time. Lower income with higher debt equals fewer choices.

the wage gap over time...

2000: For every $1 earned by a White worker, a Black worker earned **$0.90.**

2019: For every $1 earned by a White worker, a Black worker earned **$0.85.**

-Elise Gould, Economic Policy Institute, 02.27.2020

fact:

BLACK STUDENTS DEFAULT MORE OFTEN

According to the Brookings Institute, Black borrowers who graduated with a bachelor's degree defaulted on their student loans nearly five times as often their White peers. Furthermore, Black college graduates were more likely to default than White students who dropped out of college.[7]

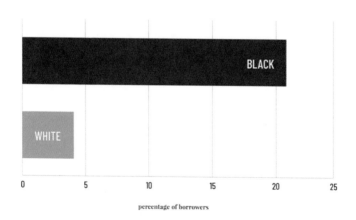

DEFAULT AMONG BACHELOR'S DEGREE GRADUATES
by race

BLACK

WHITE

| 0 | 5 | 10 | 15 | 20 | 25 |

percentage of borrowers

WHY DOES IT MATTER?

Student loan default has serious, long-term consequences which may include:

○ ENTIRE UNPAID BALANCE OF YOUR LOAN AND ANY INTEREST BECOMES DUE IMMEDIATELY.

Translation: You will be required to pay everything now. If you were unable to make a payment, then it is unlikely you will be able to pay the entire balance but that does not stop them from demanding.

○ LOSS OF ELIGIBILITY FOR DEFERMENT OR FORBEARANCE (POSTPONING REPAYMENT) AND THE ABILITY TO CHOOSE A REPAYMENT PLAN.

Translation: No more pauses in payments and no flexibility with selecting a monthly payment.

○ LOSS OF ELIGIBILITY FOR ADDITIONAL FEDERAL FINANCIAL AID.

Translation: No more grants, loans, or work-study. If you want to go back to school, you or someone else will have to pay.

○ REPORTING TO CREDIT BUREAUS, DAMAGING YOUR CREDIT RATING, AND AFFECTING YOUR ABILITY TO BORROW.

Translation: Your credit report will contain negative activity that may be viewed by lenders, employers, etc. Employers may choose not to hire you. Lenders may choose not to lend to you. If you are able to get a loan, your interest rate will likely be higher (meaning you pay back more overall).

○ TAX REFUNDS AND FEDERAL BENEFIT PAYMENTS MAY BE WITHHELD.

Translation: Your refund, social security, etc. may be seized to pay toward your debt.

○ WAGES CAN BE GARNISHED.

Translation: Your employer will send a portion of your paycheck (before you get paid) toward paying down your debt.

○ SUBJECT TO LEGAL ACTION.

Translation: You may be sued.

○ RESPONSIBLE FOR COURT COSTS, COLLECTION FEES, ATTORNEY'S FEES, AND OTHER COSTS ASSOCIATED WITH THE COLLECTION PROCESS.

Translation: If you are sued, you may have to pay for the cost of the lawsuit and the cost of them seeking payment from you.

○ YOUR SCHOOL MAY WITHHOLD YOUR ACADEMIC TRANSCRIPT

Translation: If you need an official transcript for a job or school application, the school you attended will block you from receiving one.

Source: U.S. Department of Education. Translations by author.

a sum of the parts

BORROW MORE AND BORROW MORE OFTEN

+

GRADUATE LESS OFTEN

+

MORE LIKELY TO EARN LESS

+

DEFAULT MORE FREQUENTLY

=

a problem Black borrowers cannot afford to ignore

The presentation of these facts is not meant to serve as finger-pointing at Black people. Individual behaviors and decisions have played their part, but we must acknowledge this as a systemic issue. Systemic issues can take a long time to change, and some never do, so Black borrowers cannot afford to sit back and wait on the system. You need to take control of your finances and do whatever you can to reasonably combat the outcomes I have shared. Until Black households accumulate more wealth and/or college costs decline, then students and families must be proactive to mitigate their risk of ending up like these statistics. Simply put, the mission here is more completion, less debt.

recommendations

The following recommendations are categorized by each fact and then broken out by the student's status: current student/borrower or future student. Future students should pay attention to the items listed for current borrowers as the recommendations may prove useful once you begin your education beyond high school. Also, I understand that some of these recommendations may present a challenge for many students, but if any of them are feasible then I encourage you to try them.

keys to borrowing less

COMPLETE THE FAFSA (FREE APPLICATION FOR FEDERAL STUDENT AID) AND ANY STATE FINANCIAL AID FORMS AS EARLY AS POSSIBLE IN EACH YEAR YOU PLAN TO ENROLL.

Completing the FAFSA early will not make you eligible for more federal financial aid but it may improve your chances of securing financial aid offered by your state. Complete the FAFSA before your state's priority deadline. Use the *IRS Data Retrieval Tool* to avoid making mistakes on the FAFSA as mistakes can cause delays in the approval of your financial aid and correcting mistakes can be a lengthy process.

DO NOT BORROW THE MAXIMUM AMOUNT JUST BECAUSE IT IS AVAILABLE.

Every school has a "cost of attendance" that is an estimate of how much college will cost a student for one year of attendance. The actual cost for you to attend may be less than the school's estimate. If so, borrow what you need instead of borrowing every dollar you have been offered.

TRY NOT TO SPEND FUNDS LEFTOVER AT THE END OF THE ACADEMIC YEAR.

If you have extra money from loans that you do not need, you can (1) contact your campus financial aid office to ask about a loan return. A loan return through your school can wipe out a portion of your loan and any accrued interest, or (2) borrow that much less the following year.

CONTACT THE FINANCIAL AID OFFICE IF YOUR INCOME HAS DECLINED.

Let a campus financial aid administrator know if your household income has decreased as compared to the amount listed on your FAFSA (the FAFSA uses figures from two years ago). They will let you know if the changes allow you to qualify for additional financial aid, preferably the kind that does not have to be repaid. Be mindful that many people are asking and the demand for free forms of financial aid exceeds the supply of dollars available.

BEGIN TO DEVELOP YOUR FINANCING PLAN BEFORE YOUR SENIOR YEAR OF HIGH SCHOOL.

This plan should include:
- if and how much you can afford to save.
- who (other than you) will help pay for your college expenses, how much each person will contribute, and how often the contribution will be made.
- research on free sources of funding outside of the federal government.

MAKE YOUR DECISION WITH VALUE IN MIND.

Do not hold out for the school with the best name or reputation if attending that school will place you and/or your family in financial hardship. Figure out which school will allow you to earn the credentials you need to pursue the career you want with the minimum amount of debt for you and your family.

HOW TO FIGURE OUT WHICH SCHOOL WILL COST YOU THE LEAST.

After you have been accepted, compare the financial aid offered by each school. The Consumer Financial Protection Bureau (CFPB) has a Paying for College guide that includes a free, online tool to compare financial aid offers. Visit **consumerfinance.gov** and the *Consumer Tools* section to access the guide.

tips for borrowing less often

FOLLOW THE COURSE SEQUENCE FOR YOUR MAJOR AS CLOSELY AS POSSIBLE.

An academic advisor can help you determine if you are on the path to graduate on-time. If you enroll in an extra semester, that means you will have one more semester of paying out (tuition, fees, books, etc.) as opposed to earning the salary of a college graduate.

TRY YOUR BEST TO PASS EACH CLASS THE FIRST TIME.

Every course you enroll in will cost you. There is no discount for repeats and no arrangement to pay once for unlimited attempts.

INTRODUCE YOURSELF TO YOUR CAMPUS FINANCIAL AID COUNSELOR.

Reach out and ask about scholarships and make sure your paperwork is submitted error free and on time. Also, ask about limits for the different types of aid you may have. Being aware early means if you are approaching a limit for a certain type of aid you will have the opportunity to seek other sources of funding.

There are other obvious recommendations like get a job while in school or transfer to a cheaper school, but I do not support either as a blanket recommendation for all students. Work during the terms you are out of school. As for transferring to another school, you must evaluate this on a case-by-case basis. For example, if you transfer to a cheaper school and the credits you have earned are not accepted at the school you have transferred to then it will take longer for you to graduate. Your cost savings may be negated due to the extra time needed to repeat coursework.

CHOOSE HIGHER EDUCATION AT A COLLEGE OR CAREER SCHOOL THAT ALLOWS YOU TO PURSUE YOUR CAREER GOALS WHILE KEEPING STUDENT LOAN BORROWING TO A MINIMUM FOR YOU AND YOUR FAMILY.

I recognize that this can be a daunting task, and I'll be writing another book on this very process! Here are the basics:

- Choose a career.
- Limit your search to schools that offer the academic program that will prepare you to get a job in that career.
- Narrow the list of schools by important preferences (for example: in-state vs. out-of-state, HBCU vs. PWI, face-to-face vs. online, on-campus housing vs. commuter campus). You can begin your search with **collegenavigator.gov**.
- Apply to the schools that satisfy your criteria.
- Complete the FAFSA before your state's priority deadline.
- Compare financial aid offers to determine which school will cost you and your family the least amount out-of-pocket.

CONSIDER THE SHORTEST PATHWAY TO YOUR DESIRED DEGREE OR CERTIFICATE.

Explore how to earn college credit in high school, through completing advanced placement courses or dual enrollment in a community college (taking college courses in high school).

strategies for increasing your odds of graduating

CONSULT YOUR COURSE SEQUENCE BEFORE YOU REGISTER FOR CLASSES.

Make sure the order of the courses you take (that is, the "course sequence" for your major) is aligned for you to complete in as little time as possible. Contact an academic advisor or a faculty advisor in the academic department for your major.

PAY YOUR SEMESTER BILL ON TIME.

Having an unpaid bill may prevent you from being able to register on time. Seats may fill up for a course you need to stay on track with your course sequence. Your campus policy may also call for students with unpaid balances to be dropped from classes, which means no access and no credit for any work you may have completed. Make payment arrangements with the bursar or student accounting office. Note: If financial aid funds are pending, then your campus administrators should work with you to avoid late registration and dropping your classes. Completing your FAFSA as early as possible every year can help prevent late payments. The FAFSA becomes available every year on October 1.

TAKE SOME TIME TO LEARN HOW YOU LEARN BEST.

Some people can sit through a lecture and get it the first time. Some people learn best by reading. Some people need real-life examples to connect the dots between theory and practice. Others need to learn by doing. How about you? I did not realize until graduate school that I prefer real-life examples and flash cards. I write the word on the front of a card, the definition on the back. Then, I arrange the words on a wall to see how the terms are connected. It is a lot, but it works for me. Finding what works for you will save you a lot of time and potentially money.

BUILD RELATIONSHIPS WITH FACULTY AND STAFF MEMBERS.

Stop by office hours to ask for help. Sit up straight in class. Show that you are listening or act like it even if you are not. Wait until the professor has dismissed the class to start packing up your belongings. These little things can set you apart and ensure that you are known for good reasons.

BUILD A SQUAD OR GROUP CHAT FOR EACH COURSE.

Start a group chat with your class squad and share useful information. Everyone misses a class from time to time, so arrange to get notes from someone if you must miss class and be prepared to take notes for others. Remind each other about deadlines, exams, and other important dates.

WONDERING HOW YOU LEARN BEST?

Visit **educationplanner.org** and take the "What's Your Learning Style?" self-assessment.

EXPLORE EARNING COLLEGE CREDITS WHILE IN HIGH SCHOOL.

Entering college with college credits will leave you with fewer credits to complete on campus. Some high schools offer dual enrollment for students in certain majors, which allows students to graduate high school with a high school diploma and an associate's degree.

PRIORITIZE ACADEMICS OVER WORKING, IF POSSIBLE.

If you must work while in school, try not to work so much that you have no time, energy, or mental capacity to put toward your studies. Do not pay for classes, books, etc. just to set yourself up for failure by overextending yourself.

DO NOT GO TO A SCHOOL YOU CANNOT DEVELOP A RELIABLE PLAN TO PAY FOR.

Some students go thinking they can cover the first year and figure out the rest later. This is not a practical strategy for success.

Speaking of success, your campus offers many services to support you on your journey from matriculation to completion. Use the list on the next page as a quick reference guide for who to contact based on the nature of your questions or concerns.

FOR ANSWERS OR HELP WITH	CONTACT
Your semester bill	Bursar/Student accounts
Sources of funds to pay your semester bill	Financial Aid
Course requirements and sequence for your major	Academic Advising and/or course catalog
Transferring (especially from a 2-year to a 4-year)	Academic Advising or Transfer Search for "articulation" agreements
Getting a job after school	Career services
Academic help	Tutoring and/or Writing Center
Food Insecurity	Food pantry or Student Affairs for referral to resources
Student groups including fraternities and sororities	Student Life, Greek Life, RSO Advisor (Registered Student Organization)
Athletics (student athletes)	Coach, then athletic director for referrals
Mental health/Wellness	Counseling Center
Issues with a faculty member	Department chair, then Dean, then campus leadership (Provost and/or President)
Incidents of discrimination on-campus or involving students or campus personnel (race, gender, etc.)	Title IX coordinator and other administrators as you deem necessary
Accommodations for learning and testing	Disabilities Services
Personal safety	Campus Police
Transitioning from the military (Veterans)	Bursar and/or Financial Aid for billing and benefits Student Services (the campus may have a Veterans Center)
Childcare	Student Services (for referral) College or Department of Education may have on-campus childcare
On-campus housing	Residence Life
Health care or medical issues	Student Health Center or local hospital
In-state/Out-of-state classification	Registrar or Records and Registration

proactive steps toward earning more

VISIT YOUR CAMPUS CAREER SERVICES OFFICE.

An advisor may be able to provide you with salary data for graduates. Use this information to develop a realistic estimate of salaries for people in your career and the location you plan to work in.

CONDUCT YOUR OWN FREE RESEARCH.

The U.S. Department of Labor provides salary and labor market information by career and location. You can use this information to see how many people are employed in your field in a certain location and how much they earn (on average). The OES section on the next page provides more information about how to conduct your search.

EXPLORE YOUR OPTIONS.

Do not feel compelled to accept the first job offer you receive. Many employers offer a lower salary first because they may anticipate that job applicants will return with a counteroffer (asking for more salary).

DO NOT STOP WITH SALARY, CONSIDER TOTAL COMPENSATION.

While salary is one component of the total compensation package, you can find plenty of value in other benefits like health insurance, retirement plan contributions, and continuing education benefits such as tuition remission (employer pays your tuition) and tuition reimbursement (employer pays you back for all or a portion of tuition after you successfully complete a course).

Follow the previous tips for current borrowers. You have the benefit of an earlier start; use it to your advantage. Furthermore:

BUILD AND ACCESS YOUR PERSONAL NETWORK.

Create a list of adults you know: your parents (or guardians), your friends' parents (or guardians), teachers, principals, sports coaches, etc. Think about what you can learn from each person. What do they do for a living? Where do they work? How did they get there? Did they go to college? If so, where? Identify things you have in common and things you would like to know more about. They may have knowledge or resources to share. Keep the lines of communication open by reaching out to see how they are doing and keeping them updated on your academic progress (checking in with them once per semester is a good start).

For free research on careers, credentials, and compensation, visit the Bureau of Labor Statistics **bls.gov/oes**

OES = Occupational Employment Statistics

You can browse OES Data by Occupational Profile, State or Metropolitan Area, to learn more about earnings in your career of interest. You may find it easier to begin with the Occupational Profile. Select the profile that fits your career best. Then, you can view average wages, industry profiles, and geographic profiles for the jobs you are interested in.

Be certain to explore the geography. We hear in real estate that "location is everything." Location has much to do with wages, too. For example, a finance job in New York City is likely to pay more than the same job in Atlanta. However, living in New York is likely to cost more. The cost of living may vary from one area to the next and that affects graduates in every field.

actions for decreasing your odds of default

EXERCISE YOUR RIGHT TO CHOOSE A REPAYMENT PLAN.

Your loan servicer will enroll you in the standard plan if you do not choose a plan. The required monthly payment under the standard plan is often the most expensive option because it assumes you will pay the loan off in 10 years (as opposed to 20 or 30 years). If you cannot afford the standard plan, call your servicer and ask about income-driven plans. I recommend logging in to **studentaid.gov** and using the U.S. Department of Education's *Loan Simulator* to view the options for your loans prior to contacting your servicer just to get an idea of which plan you may want to choose.

STAY IN TOUCH WITH YOUR SERVICER.

The first instinct some people have about debt is to avoid contact with the lender when they are unable to pay. Do not do this with your student loan servicer. Your servicer is working on behalf of the federal government, so they have seemingly endless methods of pursuing you for payment. Contacting them to ask for a pause or a different repayment plan can help you avoid having to experience their collections tactics.

MAXIMIZE LOAN FORGIVENESS AND/OR CANCELLATION BENEFITS.

Federal, state, and some local governments offer student loan repayment assistance. Ask a financial aid counselor at your school for information about loan forgiveness. Also visit:

- **studentaid.gov** to learn about federal loan forgiveness programs.
- the website for your state's department of education or higher education agency.
- your employer's human resources/benefits office or website.

FUTURE STUDENTS

KNOW WHAT IT MEANS TO BE A STUDENT LOAN BORROWER BEFORE YOU BORROW. Visit **studentaid.gov** and look at the Loans section to get familiar with the application requirements, loan types, loan terms, and repayment options.

CHOOSE YOUR LENDER WISELY.

This book focuses on the federal government, however some financial institutions offer "private" student loans. Private loans have borrowing and repayment terms that differ from the terms associated with federal student loans. Borrow federal loans first. If you must borrow more, then shop around for the best terms to meet your needs.

KEEP TRACK OF TIME.

Here is what you can expect after graduation. Plan ahead.

STUDENT LOAN REPAYMENT TIMELINE

EVENT	Graduation	Grace Period	Making Payments
WHEN IT BEGINS	Now	After Graduation	After grace period
WHEN IT ENDS		Usually 6 months	Your balance = zero

FINANCIAL WELLNESS FOR STUDENT LOAN BORROWERS

Do not be too hard on yourself for having student loans. Focus on managing them instead. This section provides some tips and helpful resources.

You are not alone. More than 44 million Americans have student loan debt.

Source: Federal Reserve Bank of New York Consumer Credit Panel

HOW TO DEVELOP YOUR PERSONAL STUDENT LOAN REPAYMENT STRATEGY

I recommend following four steps to develop a realistic repayment strategy that will balance the limitations of your household finances with the need to satisfy your student loan debt.

STEP 1: KNOW YOUR LOAN PORTFOLIO
STEP 2: LOCATE ANY APPLICABLE BENEFITS
STEP 3: SET YOUR REPAYMENT GOAL
STEP 4: CHOOSE YOUR REPAYMENT PLAN

STEP 1: KNOW YOUR LOAN PORTFOLIO

Visit **studentaid.gov** to obtain a list of all federal student loans that were borrowed in your name. If you borrowed loans from other sources, then you will need to obtain your credit report to see a list of all student loans.

A variety of benefits and relief programs have been designed to help student loan borrowers alleviate debt. The following list includes a sampling of sources.

FEDERAL GOVERNMENT

- **Loan forgiveness:** Visit **studentaid.gov** for information about loan forgiveness and cancellation programs including Public Service Loan Forgiveness and Teacher Loan Forgiveness.

- **Tax relief:** You may be eligible for federal tax credits and deductions related to college expenses. For example, using the Student Loan Interest Deduction may allow you to write off all or a portion of student loan interest you have paid in a given year.

STATE

Visit your state's higher education governing body or agency to locate benefits for student loan borrowers. The benefits may include state tax credits or loan repayment assistance for borrowers who work in certain locations and/or careers (this means the state will give you money to make payments toward your student loan debt).

LOCAL

Visit your city and/or county government's website. Benefits are likely limited to residents of the jurisdiction so verify that your address is within city or county limits before you apply.

EMPLOYER

Visit your employer's human resources and/or benefits website.

YOUR COLLEGE OR UNIVERSITY

Some schools offer loan repayment assistance to graduates. This is rare but worth exploring.

SERVICE-BASED

Many programs offer loan forgiveness or cancellation in exchange for time served working in a certain field and/or for a certain kind of employer. Examples include programs offered by the National Health Service Corps, Army College Loan Repayment Program (LRP) (up to $65,000), and U.S. Office of Personnel Management (OPM) which covers federal agencies.

Contrary to the calls, emails, and ads you may receive, President Obama is not going to forgive your student loans. Neither will President Trump. Their names and images are often attached to scams, so do not take the bait! If anyone contacts you and asks for your personally identifying information for student loan forgiveness, ignore them. There are legitimate organizations that provide student loan counseling which may include offering advice about student loan forgiveness. Only provide information to people you trust after you have initiated contact with them.

A final note about forgiveness: It takes time. There is no quick way to get someone else to pay off or cancel your student loan debt.

The goal for every borrower is a zero balance but there are plenty of ways to get there. I have identified three general goals: fast, forever, and forgiven.

- You can pay as much as possible as soon as possible and pay the least amount overall. I call this plan **"FAST."**
- You can pay as little as possible for as long as possible and pay the greatest amount overall. I call this plan **"FOREVER."**
- Somewhere in the middle of these two options is a plan for student loan forgiveness in which you pay as little as possible until your request for loan forgiveness or cancellation has been granted. I call this plan **"FORGIVEN."**

You should not approach student loan repayment with a "one-size fits all" mindset. Take a good look at your monthly income to compare what you are obligated to pay versus what you will earn. Repayment usually takes between 10 and 30 years so it is important to think about how repaying your student loans will fit into how you live your life.

Repayment Goal

	FAST	FORGIVEN	FOREVER
BENEFIT	Paying the least overall	Paying some, having the rest forgiven	Paying the lowest payment each month
BE MINDFUL OF	Paying the highest monthly payment	Potential tax implications Potential to temporarily restrict your options for employment (for public service loan forgiveness) PSLF is within federal law and laws may change	Paying the most overall

Exercise your right to choose a repayment plan for yourself. If you do not select a repayment plan for yourself, then your servicer will enroll you in the Standard Repayment Plan. The standard plan aligns with the "Fast" goal mentioned in Step 3. Overall, you may pay less, but the monthly payment will be the highest of your options.

WHAT WILL REPAYMENT LOOK LIKE FOR YOU?

Sample debt balance: ———————————— $30,000

What this looks like in repayment: ——— $311 PER MONTH

This example uses the Standard Repayment Plan. The Standard Repayment Plan is not feasible for some borrowers, but you must contact your servicer to select an alternative. Visit **studentaid.gov** and use the Loan Simulator to view and evaluate your options for repaying federal student loans.

Federal student loans have several repayment plans, but the plans come in two varieties: balance-driven and income-driven.

BALANCE-DRIVEN

Balance-driven plans offer a monthly payment based on the overall amount of student loans you have borrowed. These plans usually have a fixed repayment term of 10, 25, or 30 years. The amount of the monthly payment is usually fixed as well.

INCOME-DRIVEN

Income-driven plans offer a monthly payment based on what you borrowed in addition to your household finances. Every 12 months you will have to "recertify" your income-driven plan by providing proof of your adjusted gross income and family size.

The income-driven plans may provide a more affordable option, especially if you have a high amount of debt compared to your annual income. Remember: the longer you take to repay the debt, the more you are likely to pay overall. If you want to enroll in an income-driven plan, contact your servicer to verify which income-driven plans you are eligible for.

GETTING MARRIED SOON?

The REPAYE Plan considers your spouse's income as available toward repaying student loan debt regardless of how you file your taxes (joint or separately). Other income-driven plans may allow you to exclude your spouse's income if you file your taxes married, filing separately. You must decide if the lower student loan payment outweighs any tax benefits you stand to lose by filing separately. Run the numbers with tax software or consult an accountant.

The following tables from the U.S. Department of Education show how the monthly payments are calculated and for how long the payments must be made. If you have loans forgiven, then the length of repayment will be shorter.

INCOME-DRIVEN REPAYMENT PLAN	PAYMENT AMOUNT
REPAYE Plan	Generally 10 percent of your discretionary income
PAYE Plan	Generally 10 percent of your discretionary income, but never more than the 10-year Standard Repayment Plan amount
IBR Plan	Generally 10 percent of your discretionary income if you're a new borrower on or after July 1, 2014, but never more than the 10-year Standard Repayment Plan amount Generally 15 percent of your discretionary income if you're not a borrower on or after July 1, 2014, but never more than the 10-year Standard Repayment Plan amount
ICR Plan	The lesser of the following: • 20 percent of your discretionary income or • What you would pay on a repayment plan with a fixed payment over the course of 12 years, adjusted according to your income

INCOME-DRIVEN REPAYMENT PLAN	REPAYMENT PERIOD
REPAYE Plan	20 years if all loans you're repaying under the plan were received for undergraduate study 25 years if any loans you're repaying under the plan were received for graduate or professional study
PAYE Plan	20 years
IBR Plan	20 years if you're a new borrower on or after July 1, 2014 25 years if you're not a new borrower on or after July 1, 2014
ICR Plan	25 years

Source: U.S. Department of Education, studentaid.gov 3.6.2020

IF YOU HAVE NOT MISSED A PAYMENT YET BUT ARE STRUGGLING TO REPAY, CONTACT YOUR SERVICER TO

- inquire about a more affordable repayment plan. There may be a payment plan that offers a lower monthly payment. Remember, paying less each month may lead to paying more overall, but it is better to remain in good standing than to go into delinquency or default; and/or
- ask for a temporary pause in payments. Use this time to develop a realistic budget which includes making your student loan payments in full and on time, each month.

If you do not make a payment by the due date and have not contacted your servicer to make alternative arrangements, then your loans will become delinquent. Delinquency occurs before default. A delinquent status means you have missed at least one payment. Default status indicates you have missed payments for more than 270 days. If you have missed some payments but your loans are not yet in default: Contact your loan servicer to resolve the delinquency and prevent your loans from going into default.

IF YOUR STUDENT LOANS ARE IN DEFAULT

It is best to try and resolve this before the default leads to a lawsuit which may result in a judgment against you. A judgment clears the way for the lender to take a portion of your wages, benefits, etc. through a process called garnishment. Wage garnishment = cash comes out of your paycheck before your paycheck reaches you.

IF YOU HAVE **FEDERAL STUDENT LOANS:**
CONTACT YOUR SERVICER.

IF YOU HAVE **PRIVATE OR "ALTERNATIVE" LOANS:**
CONTACT YOUR LENDER.

IF YOU DO NOT KNOW WHETHER YOUR LOANS ARE IN DELINQUENCY OR DEFAULT

Contact your servicer(s) and/or login to **studentaid.gov**. You can also visit **annualcreditreport.com** to access your free credit report which should include all student loans (federal and private/alternative).

Finally, if you feel overwhelmed please seek help. Issues with debt can be complex but they can also be resolved. Visit **consumer.ftc.gov** for tips on coping with debt and working with a credit counseling organization.

"When you feel really low

Yeah, there's a great truth you should know

When you're young, gifted and black

Your soul's intact"

– NINA SIMONE

RESEARCH
AND
PHILANTHROPY

research

If you are interested in research and/or policy recommendations to address the disparities within higher education financing, the following list provides a sampling of organizations that work in this space.

CENTER FOR RESPONSIBLE LENDING	RESPONSIBLELENDING.ORG
DIGNITY + DEBT	DIGNITYANDDEBT.ORG
THURGOOD MARSHALL COLLEGE FUND	TMCF.ORG
UNITED NEGRO COLLEGE FUND	UNCF.ORG
THE EDUCATION TRUST	EDTRUST.ORG

philanthropy

As I mentioned at the beginning of the book, I was inspired to write this after watching a 2019 BET special, "Young, Gifted and Broke" hosted by Angela Rye. Having cited the inspiration, I could not close this book without acknowledging the contributions of several people who have given of themselves and/or organized efforts to alleviate the burden of student loan debt for Black students.

TOM JOYNER

(Retired radio host and Founder, the Tom Joyner Foundation)
I listened to Mr. Joyner's syndicated radio show for years. I heard many of his announcements to present HBCU students with scholarships during my morning commutes to work. According to its website, the Tom Joyner Foundation has raised more than $66 million and its awards have benefited more than 31,000 students nationwide. "The Fly Jock" recently retired from radio but shared that he will maintain his commitment to helping college students, particularly those attending HBCUs, cover college costs. For more information, visit **tomjoynerfoundation.org.**

OPRAH WINFREY

(Chairwoman and CEO, Harpo Productions and the Oprah Winfrey Network)
Oprah has invested $25 million into Morehouse College through the Oprah Winfrey Scholars Program. She has also donated to Spelman College and the United Negro College Fund.[8]

ROBERT SMITH

(Founder, Chairman, and CEO, Vista Equity Partners)
Mr. Smith, the Morehouse College Class of 2019 commencement speaker, surprised the graduates with a pledge to pay off their student loan debt. The pledge, valued at $34 million, will benefit more than 400 graduates and its provision extends to include debts borrowed by parents and guardians of the graduates.[9]

Other notable contributions have been made by Beyoncé and Jay-Z, Kevin Hart, Kenya and Dr. Rainbow Barris, Nicki Minaj, Pinky Cole and Stacey Lee, and Frank and Laura Day Baker.

conclusion

Obtaining a college degree has long been regarded as the gateway to making a stable, middle-class living. Graduates realize higher lifetime earnings, setting their lives on a higher economic trajectory which, hopefully, includes financial freedom. Unfortunately, the debt assumed while earning a degree leaves many Black borrowers feeling anything but free. Instead, they feel trapped while struggling to make ends meet.

Black students borrow more, borrow more often, graduate less often, earn less, and default more often. These facts illustrate clear racial disparities within the higher education financing system. The foundation for these disparities was cemented well before any of us set foot on a college campus. Until the foundation is shaken, we can chip away at it, one borrower at a time. Do your best to do your part.

IF YOU ARE A STUDENT LOAN BORROWER, TAKE CHARGE OF YOUR SITUATION BY SHAPING DIFFERENT OUTCOMES. YOU CAN:

- seek help if you are having trouble repaying your student loans.
- follow the four steps to developing your personal student loan repayment strategy.
- share your experience with younger students to help them make more informed decisions.
- use your voice as an advocate for systemic change through policy (engage your local, state, and federal legislators).

Being debt free, I feel free. I am free to make decisions about my future without worrying about my student loans. Decisions about my future can be made out of purpose and not out of fear. I don't take this blessing for granted.

- STEVEN G. ANDERSON II, @ANDERSONSAYS
  MOREHOUSE COLLEGE CLASS OF 2019

about the author

Tisa Silver Canady, Ed. D., MBA, is a financial wellness advocate for today's scholar. Specializing in student loan debt, she helps new borrowers think strategically about financing higher education while advising existing borrowers on their strategy to tackle, manage, and eventually eradicate their student loan debt. As an author and collegiate financial wellness expert, she has personally advised students and families on the repayment of more than $50 million in student loans.

A highly sought after thinker on personal finance, Tisa has authored personal finance content for outlets including Forbes, Investopedia, and BET. Her financial insights have been featured in radio, television, and print outlets including TIME, Ladies' Home Journal, ESSENCE Magazine, FOX Business, MSN Money, Yahoo! Finance and Maryland Public Television.

Tisa understands that graduating and starting the next chapter of your life is hard enough; being saddled with tens of thousands of dollars or more in student loan debt can make major goals like buying a house or starting a family financially impossible. Once classes end and loans come due, borrowers - especially borrowers of color - often find they didn't understand loan terms, were unaware of opportunities for loan forgiveness, don't know all the loan repayment options, and have no real plan in place to pay the money back.

Whether existing borrowers need to consolidate, identify a repayment or loan forgiveness program, Tisa works with you to understand all available options, choose the best course of action, and tackle the debt. For new borrowers, Tisa works with students and their families to understand what they can afford, develop a strategic plan to pay for college, and borrow as little as possible.

Passionate about how the student loan crisis has perpetuated a wealth gap in the African-American community, in 2020 Tisa launched **Melanin, Money, & Matriculation**, a book series and consumer education initiative. The book series includes *Borrowing While Black* and the forthcoming titles *Black Women Beyond the Bachelor's* and *When Borrowing Becomes a Family Affair*, and focuses on helping African-American borrowers make strategic decisions about student loans.

Tisa is on a mission to increase financial education around student loan borrowing. A double graduate of the University of Delaware's Alfred E. Lerner College of Business and Economics, she earned a doctorate in higher education administration/community college leadership from Morgan State University.

 **WWW.TISASILVER.COM**    **TISASILVER**   **DR.TISASILVERCANADY**

references

Judith Scott-Clayton and Jing Li. "Black-white Disparity in Student Loan Debt More Than Triples After Graduation." *Brookings Institution*, 29 Mar. 2017, www.brookings.edu/research/black-white-disparity-in-student-loan-debt-more-than-triples-after-graduation/.

The Institute for College Access & Success. 2019. Quick Facts about Student Debt. http://bit.ly/2MAXdgH.

"Pell Grants: Recipients, Maximum Pell and Average Pell – *Research* – College Board." Research, 1 Nov. 2019, research.collegeboard.org/trends/student-aid/figures-tables/pell-grants-recipients-maximum-pell-and-average-pell.

"Completing College - National by Race and Ethnicity - 2017 - **National Student Clearinghouse Research Center.**" National Student Clearinghouse Research Center, 12 June 2018, nscresearchcenter.org/signaturereport12-supplement-2/.

Carnevale, Anthony P., et al. "The College Payoff." *Georgetown University Center on Education and the Workforce*, 25 Oct. 2018, cew.georgetown.edu/cew-reports/the-college-payoff/.

Gould, Elise, et al. "Class of 2018: College Edition." *Economic Policy Institute*, www.epi.org/publication/class-of-2018-college-edition/.

Scott-Clayton, Judith. "The Looming Student Loan Default Crisis is Worse Than We Thought." *Brookings Institution,* 15 May 2018, www.brookings.edu/research/the-looming-student-loan-default-crisis-is-worse-than-we-thought/.

Amir Vera, CNN. "Oprah Donates $13 Million to Morehouse College." CNN, 8 Oct. 2019, www.cnn.com/2019/10/07/us/oprah-winfrey-morehouse-donation-trnd/index.html.

Doug Criss, CNN. "$34 Million: How Much One Man is Paying to Wipe out a Graduating Class' College Debt." CNN, 20 Sept. 2019, www.cnn.com/2019/09/20/us/morehouse-student-debt-trnd/index.html.